Una Fiesta para Pedro

por María Santos
ilustrado por Mike Dammer

Scott Foresman
is an imprint of

PEARSON

Glenview, Illinois • Boston, Massachusetts • Chandler, Arizona
Upper Saddle River, New Jersey

Every effort has been made to secure permission and provide appropriate credit for photographic material. The publisher deeply regrets any omission and pledges to correct errors called to its attention in subsequent editions.

Unless otherwise acknowledged, all photographs are the property of Pearson.

Photo locations denoted as follows: Top (T), Center (C), Bottom (B), Left (L), Right (R), Background (Bkgd)

Illustrations by Mike Dammer

8 ©Jim Gaigmyle/Corbis

ISBN 13: 978-0-328-53334-3
ISBN 10:   0-328-53334-3

Copyright © by Pearson Education, Inc., or its affiliates. All rights reserved. Printed in the United States of America. This publication is protected by copyright, and permission should be obtained from the publisher prior to any prohibited reproduction, storage in a retrieval system, or transmission in any form or by any means, electronic, mechanical, photocopying, recording, or likewise. For information regarding permissions, write to Pearson Curriculum Rights & Permissions, One Lake Street, Upper Saddle River, New Jersey 07458.

Pearson® is a trademark, in the U.S. and/or other countries, of Pearson plc or its affiliates.

Scott Foresman® is a trademark, in the U.S. and/or other countries, of Pearson Education, Inc., or its affiliates.

2 3 4 5 6 7 8 9 10 V0N4 13 12 11 10

Pedro está feliz. Por fin es sábado.
—Tu fiesta saldrá muy linda —dice su madre.
—Todo está listo desde el martes o miércoles —dice su padre.

Pedro abre una caja grande como un cofre. Francis grita: —¡Sorpresa!

Su hermana Andrea dice: —Mi hermano, compré tu regalo el jueves.

Ahora Pedro se enfrenta a la piñata.
¡Dale duro, Pedro, que no es frágil!

Es hora de comer. Todos disfrutan de los tacos de la abuelita Frida. Luego habrá pastel de fresa.

Los músicos tocan "Las mañanitas"
y todos cantan.
—¡Qué fiesta tan linda! —dice Pedro—.
¡Gracias a mis padres y a todos!

Las piñatas

Leamos juntos

Hay piñatas de distintas formas, tamaños y colores. Se llenan de golosinas y juguetes pequeños. Las piñatas son una tradición en México y otros países de América Latina. Cada día es más común verlas en fiestas de cumpleaños que se celebran en los Estados Unidos.